MW00901310

Guest Book to Celebrate

Guests

Name ______________________________

Message ______________________________

____

____

____

____

____

____

____

Name ______________________________

Message ______________________________

____

____

____

____

____

____

____

Guests

Name ______________________

Message ______________________

Name ______________________

Message ______________________

Guests

Name ______________________

Message ______________________

____

____

____

____

____

____

____

Name ______________________

Message ______________________

____

____

____

____

____

____

____

Guests

Name

Message

Name

Message

Guests

Name ____________________________

Message ____________________________

Name ____________________________

Message ____________________________

Guests

Name

Message

Name

Message

Guests

Name

Message

Name

Message

Guests

Name

Message

Name

Message

Guests

Name

Message

Name

Message

Guests

Name ______________________

Message ______________________

____

____

____

____

____

____

____

Name ______________________

Message ______________________

____

____

____

____

____

____

____

Guests

Name ______________________

Message ______________________

____

____

____

____

____

____

____

Name ______________________

Message ______________________

____

____

____

____

____

____

____

Guests

Name

Message

Name

Message

Guests

Name ______________________

Message ______________________

Name ______________________

Message ______________________

Guests

Name

Message

Name

Message

Guests

Name

Message

Name

Message

Guests

Name ______________________

Message ______________________

Name ______________________

Message ______________________

Guests

Name

Message

Name

Message

Guests

Name

Message

Name

Message

Guests

Name

Message

Name

Message

Guests

Name ______________________

Message ______________________

____

____

____

____

____

____

____

Name ______________________

Message ______________________

____

____

____

____

____

____

____

Guests

Name ________________________________

Message ________________________________

____

____

____

____

____

____

____

Name ________________________________

Message ________________________________

____

____

____

____

____

____

____

Guests

Name

Message

Name

Message

Guests

Name

Message

Name

Message

Guests

Name

Message

Name

Message

Guests

Name

Message

Name

Message

Guests

Name

Message

Name

Message

Guests

Name

Message

Name

Message

Guests

Name ______________________

Message ______________________

____

____

____

____

____

____

____

Name ______________________

Message ______________________

____

____

____

____

____

____

____

Guests

Name

Message

Name

Message

Guests

Name ______________________

Message ______________________

____

____

____

____

____

____

____

Name ______________________

Message ______________________

____

____

____

____

____

____

____

Guests

Name ______________________

Message ______________________

____

____

____

____

____

____

____

Name ______________________

Message ______________________

____

____

____

____

____

____

____

Guests

Name

Message

Name

Message

Guests

Name ____________________

Message ____________________

Name ____________________

Message ____________________

Guests

Name

Message

Name

Message

Guests

Name

Message

Name

Message

Guests

Name

Message

Name

Message

Guests

Name

Message

Name

Message

Guests

Name

Message

Name

Message

Guests

Name

Message

Name

Message

Guests

Name

Message

Name

Message

Guests

Name

Message

Name

Message

Guests

Name

Message

Name

Message

Guests

Name ____________________

Message ____________________

____

____

____

____

____

____

____

Name ____________________

Message ____________________

____

____

____

____

____

____

____

Guests

Name

Message

Name

Message

Guests

Name ______________________

Message ______________________

Name ______________________

Message ______________________

Guests

Name

Message

Name

Message

Guests

Name

Message

Name

Message

Guests

Name ______________________

Message ______________________

____

____

____

____

____

____

____

Name ______________________

Message ______________________

____

____

____

____

____

____

____

Guests

Name

Message

Name

Message

Gift List

Guests	Gifts

Gift List

Guests	Gifts

Gift List

Guests	Gifts

Gift List

Guests	Gifts

Gift List

Guests	*Gifts*

Gift List

Guests	Gifts

Gift List

Guests	Gifts

Gift List

Guests	Gifts

Gift List

Guests	Gifts

Gift List

Guests	Gifts

Gift List

Guests	Gifts

Made in the USA
Monee, IL
14 May 2022